GABRIEL FAURE

Messe Basse
& other sacred works

for female or boys' voices
& organ or piano

Edited by Desmond Ratcliffe

Order No: NOV 030136

NOVELLO PUBLISHING LIMITED

CONTENTS

The durations shewn above are approximate.

EDITORIAL NOTE

All English words, unless stated otherwise, have been translated or adapted by the editor. The use of square brackets denotes editorial additions, but Man. and Ped. indications are suggestions only. The accompaniment to the *Cantique de Jean Racine* has been labelled Piano or Organ and not vice versa as it seems so pianistic.

D.R. 1977

MESSE BASSE

KYRIE ELEISON

20202

2

4

SANCTUS

BENEDICTUS

AGNUS DEI

Ag - nus_ De - i qui_ tol -
Lamb of_ God who takes a -

lis pec - ca - ta mun di,_ mi - se - re - re
way the sins_ of the world,_ have_ mer - cy

no - bis,_ mi - se - re - re no - bis._
on us,_ have_ mer - cy on us._

* Lower notes are for piano

14

à Monsieur César Franck

CANTIQUE DE JEAN RACINE

Opus 11

English words by
Sarah Leftwich*

PIANO
or ORGAN

* By permission

34 Man.

37

pp

Ped.

[p] dolce

Ré - pands sur
Shed o - ver

[p] dolce

Ré - pands sur
Shed o - ver

[p]

40

nous le feu de ta grâ - ce puis - san - te, Que
us the fire of thy strength and thy com - fort, May

nous le feu de ta grâ - ce puis - san - te, Que
us the fire of thy strength and thy com - fort, May

43

55

Qui la con - duit à l'ou-bli de tes lois, ___
Which cau - ses it to for-get thy de - cree, ___

duit ___ à l'ou - bli de _ tes _ lois,
it ___ to for - get thy_ de - cree,

58

Qui la con - duit à l'ou-bli de tes
Which cau - ses it to for-get thy de -

Qui la con - duit ___ à l'ou - bli de tes
Which cau - ses it ___ to for - get thy de -

61

lois!
cree!

lois!
cree!

O Christ sois fa - vo - rable à ce
O Christ, look down with fa - vour on

sempre legato

Man.

peu - ple fi - dè - le, Pour te bé -
those__ who a - dore__ thee, To bless thy

64

nir main - te - nant ras - sem - blé,
name we are ga - thered, O Lord,

67

Ped.

p
Re -
Re -

çois les chants qu'il of - fre à ta gloire im - mor -
ceive the songs we of - fer to thy e - ter - nal

p
Re - çois les chants qu'il of - fre à ta gloire
Re - ceive the songs we of - fer to thy e -

cresc.

cresc.

70

24

82 Man.

Ped.

85

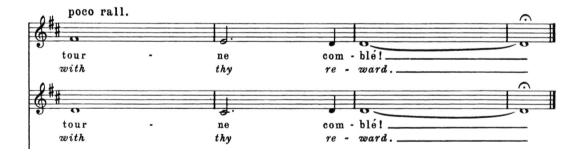

88

MARIA, MATER GRATIAE

Opus 47, No. 2

26

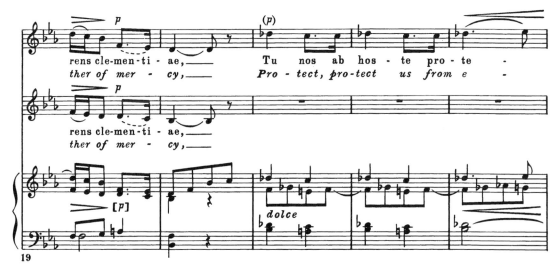

20202

28

Spi - ri - tu, In_ sem-pi - ter - nam, sem-pi-ter-nam sae - cu - la,
Spi_ rit, *For e_ ver, for_ e - ver and e - ver,*

Spi - ri - tu,_ In_ sem-pi - ter - nam, sem-pi-ter-nam sae - cu - la,
Spi_ rit,_ *For e_ ver, for_ e - ver and e - ver,*

44 Ped.

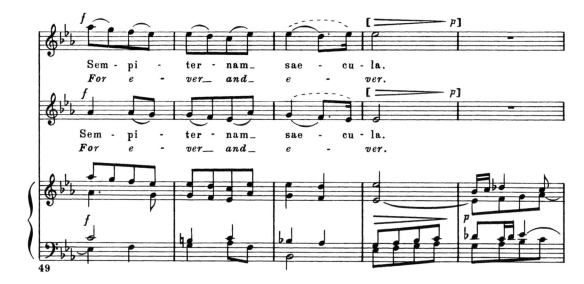

Sem - pi - ter - nam_ sae - cu - la.
For e - ver_ and_ e - ver.

Sem - pi - ter - nam_ sae - cu - la.
For e - ver_ and_ e - ver.

49

A - men,____ A - men.____
A - men,____ *A - men.____*

A - men,____ A - men.____
A - men,____ *A - men.____*

54

AVE VERUM

Opus 65, No. 1

Ve-re pas-sum, im-mo-la-tum In_ cru-ce pro ho-mi-ne.
On the cross thy sa-cred Bo-dy For us_ men with nails was torn.

Cu-jus la-tus
Cleanse us, by the

14
Ped.

un - da flu - xit, un-da
wa - ter Stream ing, streaming

cresc.

per - fo-ra-tum un-da flu - xit cum san-gui - ne,__ un-da
blood and wa-ter Stream-ing__ from thy pier-ced Side, streaming

cresc.

19

flu - xit cum san - gui-ne; Es-to no-bis
from thy__ pier - ced Side; Feed us with thy

flu - xit cum san - gui-ne;
from thy__ pier - ced Side;

23
Man.

re - re, mi-se - re - re. A - men,
on us, have mer - cy. A - men,

mi - se - re - re.
mer - cy on us.

52

A - - men,
A - - men,

A - men,
A - men,

56

[dim.] pp
A - men.
A - men.

[dim.] pp
A - men.
A - men.

[dim.]

60

TANTUM ERGO

Opus 65, No. 2

St Thomas Aquinas, 1227-1274
Translated by J. M. Neale,
E. Caswall, and others

36

15

19

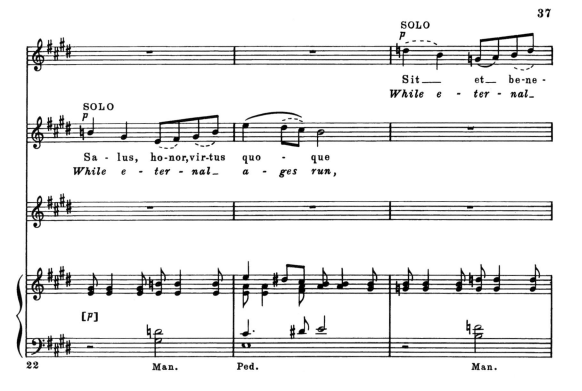

Com-par_ sit_ lau - da-ti-o, Com-par_ sit_ lau - da-ti-o.
Who from both, with both is one, Who from both, with both is one.

Com-par_ sit_lau - da-ti-o,___ Com-par sit lau - da-ti-o.
Who from both, with both is one,_ Who from both, with both is one.

Com-par_ sit_ lau - da-ti-o, Com-par sit lau - da-ti-o.
Who from both, with both is one, Who from both, with both is one.

28

A - men,___ A - men,___ A - men, A - men.
A - men,___ A - men,___ A - men, A men.

A - men,___ A - men,___ A - men, A - men.
A - men,___ A - men,___ A - men, A men.

A - men,___ A - men,___ A - men, A - men.
A - men,___ A - men,___ A - men, A men.

A - men, A - men, A - men.
A - men, A - men, A men.

[dolce]   [PP]

32

AVE MARIA

Opus 67, No. 2

poco a poco cresc.

dic - ta tu in mu - li - e - ri-bus, et be - ne -
bless - ed art thou a - mong wo - men,and bless - ed,

poco a poco cresc.

12

dic - tus fruc - tus ven - tris tu - i,
bless - ed is___ the fruit of thy womb,___

16

Je - sus.___ Sanc - ta Ma - ri - a, Ma - ter
Je - sus.___ Ho - ly Ma - ry, Mo - ther of

20

cresc.

De - i, o - ra, o - ra pro no - bis pec-ca-to-ri -
God,___ pray for us sin-ners,pray for us__ sin -

cresc.

24

bus,   nunc et   in   ho -   ra   mor -   tis
ners,   now,   and   at   the   hour of   our

nos -   trae,   nunc et in   ho -   ra mor-tis   nos
death,   now,   and   at   the   hour   of our

trae.   A   -   -   men,
death.   A   -   -   men,

A   -   -   men.
A   -   -   men.

Novello Publishing Limited
Printed in Great Britain by Caligraving Limited, Thetford, Norfolk.

CHORAL MUSIC FOR FEMALE AND BOYS' VOICES

BLYTON, Carey
LADIES ONLY
Five songs for unaccompanied SSA

BRAHMS
SONGS OF LOVE
Arranged for SSA & piano. Piano duet
accompaniment on sale.

FAURE
arr Desmond Ratcliffe
MESSE BASSE & OTHER SACRED WORKS
For SSA & piano or organ
arr Desmond Ratcliffe
REQUIEM
For SBar (or SA) soli, SSA chorus & orchestra

HOLST
SEVEN PART-SONGS
For SSA & strings

HURD, Michael
CHARMS & CEREMONIES
For unison voices, S(S)A & piano or string
orchestra
FLOWER SONGS
For S(S)A & string orchestra or piano
MISSA BREVIS
For SSA & organ or piano or string orchestra
THREE SAINTS IN ONE
For SSA, flute (optional) & piano

MENDELSSOHN
arr Cilla Dennis
HYMN OF PRAISE
For SSA

PERGOLESI
STABAT MATER
For SA soli, SA chorus & orchestra

PHILIPS, John
EIGHT NEGRO SPIRITUALS
Arranged for unaccompanied SSA

PURCELL
arr Maurice Blower
COME YE SONS OF ART
For SSA & piano or strings

SALLINEN, Aulis
SONG AROUND A SONG
For unaccompanied children's chorus (SSA)

STAINER
arr Desmond Ratcliffe
CRUCIFIXION
For TB (or SA) soli, SSA chorus & organ

VIVALDI
arr Desmond Ratcliffe
GLORIA
For SSA, trumpet in C, oboe, strings & organ